I0135375

Ruth Bavetta

SELECTED POEMS

FUTURECYCLE PRESS

www.futurecycle.org

Cover photo by Ruth Bavetta; cover and interior design by Diane Kistner;
Gentium Book Basic text and Cronos Pro titling

Library of Congress Control Number: 2023946851

Copyright © 2023 Ruth Bavetta
All Rights Reserved

Published by FutureCycle Press
Athens, Georgia, USA

ISBN 978-1-952593-50-5

Contents

Foreword

from
FLOUR, WATER, SALT

from
NO LONGER AT THIS ADDRESS

from
WHAT'S LEFT OVER

OTHER POEMS

from
WINTER SLEEP OVER

OTHER POEM

Foreword

Some poets we remember for a few spectacular poems, some poets we remember for the cumulative power of their body of work. A few poets offer both. What a pleasure it is to open a book by Ruth Bavetta and know that every poem will be a joy to read.

It is not an exaggeration to say Ruth Bavetta is a polymath. Her education and interests are wide-ranging. She holds a BS in Geology/Paleontology, a BA in Art, an MFA in Painting. She ran a chemistry lab, was a suburban housewife with kids, taught Drawing and Art History at the college level, showed her paintings in a Los Angeles area art gallery. After taking a writing workshop, she turned her deep curiosity about the workings of the world to the art of poetry.

Bavetta is a master of both formal and free verse. She is equally at home in the villanelle as she is in the lyrical narrative, or the short imagistic poem. Since she began her artistic life as a painter, it is natural that many of her early poems are ekphrastic. The poem "Bay," responding to a Claire Browne drawing, begins with these three lines, which set the rhyme scheme for the musical, evocative poem that follows:

> She draws tiny circles one by one with her left hand.
> They foam across the canvas like bubbles on the beach
> roll and effervesce across the sand.

If art is long and life is short, sometimes the artist must change her life. In twenty-one short lines from "How to Get There," we get the gist of the story. The following lines are from the middle of the poem:

> Six months after I met him, I left
> my house, my street, my town, steering
> books, socks, dogs, cats, kids
> from their known coordinates right
> across the valley to this house where

The poet begins the next passionate chapter of her life. Her lyric poetry explodes in joy and wonder, even after the loss of her great love. The poem "Corpus," begins:

> This body, this boat I've sailed on

is an ode to the body itself, the vehicle in which we all live, and which we all must ultimately abandon. The body of Ruth Bavetta's work is spectacular.

—Donna Hilbert,
author of *Threnody,* Moon Tide Press, 2022

from
FUGITIVE PIGMENTS

FutureCycle Press, 2013

Memories Suspended by Filaments

—in the voice of Joseph Cornell

The house is small, but it has room for dreams.
For birds, books, stamps, stars, marbles, butterflies,
balls, dolls, my brother Robert, maps, romance,
playing cards, lace, lobsters, small sticky hope.

Eyes down, I walk the streets of Manhattan,
eat pastries, sweet, stale, talk to pigeons, find
orphaned desires in gutters, in dime stores,
in second-hand shops with dusty windows.

I discover, gather, magpie away.
My treasures hibernate waiting, sleeping
in basement shelf rows, labeled by heartbeats
slowed to a drip. When my dossiers have lived

together long enough, I take them out,
let them speak, cherish them in my boxes,
where parrots talk of sunsets, and clay pipes
float and fill with a summer of bubbles.

Behind glass, my birds and my women sing,
locked into universes I create,
where lovers are dancers, princesses, queens,
secrets detained in shining glass bottles.

I sing the *juene fille* Lauren Bacall,
slender Botticelli, silent in blue,
construct a pink palace with sapphire stars.
I mediate history for the Prince

of the Medici, give him a compass
so he finds and he follows true love. Oh,
Bebe Marie, you are so beautiful,
pale pink, hidden among silvery twigs.

Dear as Salt

—on Ralph Going's painting, *Double Ketchup, 1996-97*

The salt stands iconic on the counter
guardianed by blood-red double ketchups,
flooded with light flowing from the right.

Sodium chloride, a molecule of two,
each harmful alone, when bonded
together they live in harmony.

Halite, hexoctahedral, isometric, perfect
cleavage. Here are pure white cubic crystals
sparkling in a stubby glass shaker

on a diner counter. Sought and sold for seasoning,
medicine, taxes, ketchup, the mining of silver.
Preservative for Egypt's everlasting dead.

The Princess told her father,
you are as dear to me as salt
and he, offended to be compared

to such a commonplace, threatened
to banish her from the palace. Until
she served him roast bream and darioles,

mustard soup, simnel cake, Swithin cream,
pasties filled with marrow, all without salt,
tasteless as a life without love.

Salt makes it harder for things to boil
and harder too, for them to freeze,
prevents the yeast from overflowing.

From mines, from brines, from solar heat,
symbol of fertility, symbol of purity,
regulator of the heart.

Salt is ancient, salt is eternal.
Salt is what he offers me
every night across the table.

Atelier

—for my grandmother, Edna Rosalie Tuttle Pomeroy

Turpentine
mineral spirits
casein
glycerin
Let me go to her
in memory, watch
her prepare the canvas.
gesso
fresco
lead white
graphite
In the aftertimes,
she's a last dream
rose madder
before waking.
cerulean
cadmium
cobalt
High at the window,
morning
glazing
the apple,
and in her studio,
porcelain enamel
her first cup of tea.

What Is Left to Show That I Was Here?

Remember me in the Ultramarine
of an empty bed, find me
in the Cardinal Purple
of a canceled stamp, the Marking Blue
of builders, handsaws, teachers. Viridian
of rooms webbed with birds.
I will be in the Cadmium Red
of random apples, in the Burnt
Umber basket of a shadow. Vermilion
will account for a puncture
in the skin of loneliness.
Look for me in the Aurelian pollen
of Cerulean lilacs, in the ache
of Mars Violet. Bone Black crows
on branches, Alizarin Crimson to weep
and soak my shirt.
Lamp Black.
Cardinal purple.
Caput mortuum.

Colors and Outlines

—for Ann

Ever since the last
biopsy, she has known
she is not safe, has never
been safe, from the invisible
procession of cells.
Since that day, when the ache
passed from the imaginary
to the real, she has been naked
beneath her skin.

The newspaper, carelessly flung
near her mailbox, brings reports
she cannot read. She counts
only April speeding past. Her last
pennies are about to be spent.
She will let them go
as she has let go of the desire
to get into her car
and just keep driving.

Still Life with Pencil

The book
you were reading last night,
the old green flashlight
your grandmother kept
under her pillow,
the carving knife
bought by your former husband—
look how your fingers
curl around them. The key
to your first house,
a beautiful, but empty pen,
the ball of the thumb
you have taken for granted
your entire life, the astonishing curve
of your fingernails. These are the things
you will draw from.

Red

is a broken pomegranate
spilling blood and rubies
onto salt-white linen;

a shattered glass of burgundy;
maraschino cherries,
the sticky lips
of a teenage siren.

It is a Chinese leather box,
a Hungarian Rhapsody,
the taste of *sachertorte,*
a spill of rouge
in a dim and shuttered room.

Bay

—Claire Browne, 2000, colored pencil on canvas, 12x12 inches

She draws tiny circles one by one with her left hand.
They foam across the canvas like bubbles on the beach
roil and effervesce across the sand.

Colored pencil circles done freehand
on gesso sanded clean and white as bleach,
drawn one by one with her left hand.

A mitosis of new cells, bacteria, a strand
of stars, thousands come together, leach
their efflorescence from the sand.

A spume of blues and greens fanned
as distant from the past as she can reach
drawing round and round with her left hand.

Creeping over bounds and edges, contraband
reflections crawl across the canvas, pleached
with roils and effervescence on the sand.

She transcends a childhood she did not understand,
closes memories away without their speech,
as tiny circles fall one by one from her left hand
and they roil and effloresce across the sand.

Running Fence

—Christo, Sonoma County, California, 1976

Improbable as a line of laundry,
indispensable as a spine,
a lightning bolt
that celebrates the contour of hills,
it fades into fog, rises into sun.
A dash of chalk against the summer brown,
describing the wind,
it disappears into a valley, reappears
on the hill, curves
over a crest, gone,
returned
to plunge
at last
into the sea.

To Make a Mark

Emptiness is deadly. To master it
you must blemish it. A long slashing
line, a curve curling back
upon itself, a line that winds
with no end in mind.

Once you have destroyed perfection
you will be entering
a country you have not known.
I will not tell you this.

You may find something amazing—
someone to take your hand, a waterfall,
a fall from three flights up.
I will not tell you this, either.

I will tell you only that it doesn't matter
if, by the end, your first mark
has disappeared. It matters only
that you have made it.
Pick up your pencil now.
Begin.

First Lesson

Even Rembrandt's paintings
didn't all end up in a museum.
Some he scraped off and painted over.
Others he pitched into the canal,
along with his debts and bad teeth.
But the debts recurred,
the teeth gave him bad breath,
the canal gurgled and disturbed his sleep.

Picasso drew on napkins to pay his bar tab.
But even when he worked on hot-pressed,
acid-free, pure linen paper,
he sometimes trampled his drawings
or folded them into airplanes
to sail at the heads of his wives and mistresses.

Leonardo couldn't get the smile right.
Not the first time. Nor the second.
Georgia painted a world of bones,
deserts, and high, wide spaces—
and a world of paintings
she should have had the sense to burn.

Van Gogh's early drawings
were stiff and awkward—
no coiling sunflowers, no writhing skies,
no cypresses twisting toward the stars.
Did you think this was going to be easy?

The Annunciation

—Simone Martini, 1333

Mary twists to stare at the intruder,
an Angel, no less. His plaid-lined cape
flutters, lifted by a breeze
that touches nothing else. Waxy lilies,
white and virginal, spring from a vase.

She turns away, clutches her robe
of ultramarine and gold across her breast
as if she's been caught undressed.
She's stuck her thumb into her book
so she won't lose her place.
Her mouth turns down.

She sees it even now—the birth out of town
in dismal lodgings, swaddling clothes, damp
and odorous, husband resentful
of a child not his own, the embarrassing ruckus
in the temple, the motley gang of followers,
the agonizing and ignominious death,
the sponge soaked in vinegar.

Adagio

A slow stroll eased
into three syllables not four,
for G and I are married

into one soft sound.

A sweet plum
of a word, slide it

across the spoon
of your tongue.

Let it repeat,

a bell slowly tolling from beyond
three valleys, carrying

a calm the color of gold dust.

Slide into the susurrus
of faraway surf.

Pianissimo, pianissimo.

When the Room Fades

I want the orange felt hat,
the silver brush, the notebook
with the broken back.
I want Los Angeles, Encino,
San Bernardino, the overflow
of pages, the tangle of pins,
all those things I've carried
wrapped in the silk of living.

I want the shoes, sunglasses,
broken seashells, the lilies,
lawns and clothes lines.
The slow decay
of lilacs, swift summer
stars against a sinking sky.
I want just one single minute
to carry like a peach pit
in my deepest pocket.

Luncheon on the Grass

—Eduard Manet, 1863

Two young men
lounge on the grass,
black jackets, spotless trousers.
Next to them, a naked woman.

Another woman, wearing only
her shimmy, dabbles in the pond.
Picnic basket, overturned,
spills ripe fruit, golden bread.

The men absorbed in discussion—
philosophy, stock market, horses—
haven't even removed their cravats,
or tasted the food the women brought.

The naked woman's feet are muddy,
perhaps she's just come from a dip
beside her sister. Instead of listening
to the men, she stares out at us.

So? She says, when was your last picnic?
When did you last strip down
and turn your muddy feet to view?
In a minute, she'll reach out
and bite into one of those peaches.

Camera degli Sposi (The Bridal Chamber)

—ceiling fresco, Andrea Mantegna, 1474

Afterwards, we lie on the bed,
limbs flung wide, my kirtle, his *doppieto*
on the floor, tangled with the wedding
silks, our sweaty bodies far apart,

breathing hard, but not in unison.
The ceiling above me is a painted balustrade
around a painted hole, a painted sky
strewn with painted clouds.

It's like being at the bottom of a well.
Outside, it could be raining—
lightning, thunder, stars darkening,
but in this room the sky is always blue.

What a crowd up there around the edge—
all those merry cherubs, a dark man in a turban,
several women staring, even a bird.
I feel like I should cover up.

The cherubs have fat, creased thighs,
stubby little penises. The man cocks
his head. The bird gazes at the clouds,
as if overtaken by yearning.

Below, on rumpled sheets
of fine-woven linen, I touch his shoulder.
That bird, I ask, is it a pheasant?
He looks, rolls away from me.

Idiota, he says, it's a peacock.
I want to stroke the soft hair
curling at the back of his neck
but I don't dare. Instead, I look up.

On the balustrade
between two women, is a heavy tub
filled with greenery, balanced
on the very edge.

Self-portrait

—Alice Neel, 1980, oil on canvas

Eighty you are, Alice, planted
in a blue-striped chair, more naked
than nude. In one hand you hold a brush
like a baton, as if conducting your life,
in the other, a rag for wiping out mistakes.

Your breasts, like mine, droop
over an abdomen poured like a land slump
onto plump thighs. Pizza, pregnancies,
peanut butter, whiskey, long sweet afternoons
in the studio instead of in the gym.

Turkey neck, jowls, marriage, divorce,
paint under the fingernails. I see myself
with the same down-turned mouth,
the same skeptical stare and wonder
how we got our bodies through it all.

You used to say an empty chair by the window
would be your only self portrait. Save
that chair for me, Alice. I'm drawing close.
Tell me how to come ashore.

from
EMBERS ON THE STAIRS

Moontide Press, 2014

West of Reno

1

Driving up old Gold Lake Road
we dodged lumber trucks
careening unpaved curves at heedless speed.
Sometimes they carried but a single log,
one arboreal body so huge
it could not share its coffin,

a trunk that had survived winter storms,
August thirst, September fire,
only to have its majesty laid out,
carried in a breakneck funeral procession
to the lumber mill at Sattley.

Whatever we can learn
from the now-abandoned mill,
the rusted cone which once burned
the dust of trees like these, is offset
by our tendency to prefer roads clear
and paved, wherever they may lead.

2

Last year we drove to Johnsville, set up
the telescope, stared at whirling galaxies
where no point is fixed,
where stars roam untethered
by charts and expectations.

Something forces us to search
for what attaches us to earth,
to the keening needles of the pines,
water-eaten cliffs abandoned
by hydraulic miners, sound
distilled to tumbled fragments.

We cling to tender surfaces,
the ever-present wind against us.
Riffles cross the lake
broken, mended, broken.

Autumn Sacrifice

When I bring the pomegranates into the kitchen,
already my hands are stained with red.
The bruised globes, with their gaping wounds,
ooze crimson onto the white tiles.

The hard dry skins resist my knife.
A slip, and my blood mingles with the fruit's.
Cooked with sugar, thickened, poured into jars,
the jelly is both sweet and bitter.

Afghanistan

There is only this stain
only this growing fist
of poppies, only these birds that gain
the cliffs of winter. Just these avenues that hang
beside a well. Somewhere a stag
dies on a plain, then dies again.
Summer's air suffers with the tang
of the lost faith
of children. This is the gist
of all the songs we sang.
This is all that we began. This.

How to Get There

I'm no good
at giving directions, always forget
the names of streets,
just point myself the right
way, past the big green house
turn left at the tall brick wall,
right at the street heading out.
Six months after I met him, I left
my house, my street, my town, steering
books, socks, dogs, cats, kids
from their known coordinates right
across the valley to this house, where
we've lived for thirty years, twenty
since the children grew and left. Even
now I can't tell you the right way
to get where you're going.
Once you've left,
go right on down the street
and when you get to the place
where you need to turn,
turn.

Sixty-Seven years

and I've understood nothing
except the stretched weight of summer nights,
the burn of the sun at four o'clock,
the shadows of the eucalyptus,
the indifference of rain.
I wait for clouds to arrive from the west,
for my teeth, hair, skin,
bones, fingernails to thin;
and the sky smells of melting candles,
and the trees are still.

Addictions

I love books.
When I go into a bookstore
I try not to lose control,

but then I tell myself
buying another book
doesn't really count as
spending money.

Just like when I eat
standing up in the kitchen,
the calories aren't real calories
and would never make me fat.

Learning something new
is the most exciting thing I know,
better than sex, almost,

but sex
I can do
without my glasses.

Ode to Menopause

The lunar tide fades,
a wound known only
by its absence.
The cart in the market
passes the packets
of tampons and pads.
Liberty's unlocked
the balance
of white against scarlet.
Loosed from the calendar,
a cup of red
containing no red,
no condoms, no jelly
no pills, no diaphragm,
no fruit of desire
but desire itself.

Oranges and Pomegranates

I'm tired of hearing about weathered barns
and cows and icy Vermont winters.
Sometimes it seems that every poet in America
lives on a farm in New England. Enough

already, give me someone who sings of golden hills
dehydrated under an August sun, of sage
and chaparral, eucalyptus and red-tailed hawks,
and crummy motels hooded with bougainvillea.

Tell me of freeways wide as the Plains of Abraham,
interchanges thicketed like mangrove swamps,
and tides of tile-roofed houses spread out
in mortgaged blots across the land.

Spin songs of palms and pyracantha, of olives
and oranges and pomegranates, of beaches
tawdry with bottles and cigarette butts,
and the smell of sprinklers on a sun-baked sidewalk.

Let me see Latinos in white straw hats selling oranges
at the freeway offramps while ghost coyotes nip
at the tasseled edges of the city. I crave the pure,
magnificent, bloody beauty of a smoggy sunset.

Poured Melting from the Dark

In the shadow of the mountain
chrysanthemums of flame unfurl
like a lover's insults.

Deneb wheels overhead,
an evolving conversation
between dream and blaze.

The light of burning stars
hurls its blistering breath
roiling over the hills, sowing

a feathery fantasy of ashes.
Sirens from the east, distant wails
poured melting from the dark.

Wind blooms with gritty sparkles,
spins over the hill and beyond.
Everything bright arrives in waves.

Sewing Lessons

—for my aunts, Rosalie and Catherine

I come from the school of stitches,
the lace of Sicily, slender strings
under a child's tired fingers,

a misplaced strand of silk.

I come from the voyage of seams,
Santa Margherita, New York, Los Angeles.

I come from young women, bent over
power machines, fording the river of cloth.

I come from learning to say needle for *ago,*
thread for *filo,* Charlie instead of *Calogero.*

I come from basting the pieces together,
following patterns, matching designs,

cutting away the unwanted to form the new.

I come from struggling to suture the fabric,
line for line, dot for dot, notch for notch,
so the seams can hardly be seen.

Elegy for Aunt Katie

Whatever seam you worked on,
there were always needles,
and the almost invisible

threads that clung to you
as you guided the cloth
with your small fingers,

cramming wool, silk, cotton,
under the jaws of the power machine,
another, another, another,

until your wrists ached
and at the end of the day
your knees would not unbend.

This is goodbye.

You lie in St. Dominic's Church,
with candles, incense, gilt,
where Father Mark embraced you,

Sister Agnes told you the Inquisition
was only a few bad priests,
benedictam, adscriptam, ratam, rationabilem,

where all you could have known
was held at bay
by all that you believed.

Your heart lies like an apple
in the center of the City of the Angels.
Per omnia sæcula sæculorum. Amen.

Settling Accounts

He has a mouth like a bankbook,
all he has to do is open it
and I disagree with him,
whether I do or not.

He's a crisp, white shirt, a wingtip
shoe, a black and white TV,
neat, tidy, cool. Chocolate
wouldn't melt in his hand.

He thumbs through rows
of folders, everything catalogued,
not a bungalow, a child, an ambulance,
a morning, out of place.

He knows where apples belong, paintings
and penitentiaries, butterflies and blood.
Whenever he sees me, he looks up from his ledger
and hands me a paper clip.

Fishing Lesson

—after Alan Shapiro

Two fishermen rest their elbows
on the railing of the pier, looking out.
The older of the two is saying how strange
it is to realize the ocean goes past the horizon
all the way to China and up and down
from the north pole to the south pole.
I bet you could sail for a hundred years,
he tells the other, and never set foot on land.

Behind them, a woman too old to be so blonde
walks with her son, or maybe he's not her son.
From the bait shack the music of Green Day
curls around umbrellas, toddlers, chess players.
The younger fisherman is thinking
only of his line, and where it goes deep
into the dark water, how the bit of anchovy
he's jammed onto the hook
is sending waves of fishy deliciousness
into the water, summoning tonight's dinner.

At the base of the cliffs the train rumbles
past the pizza place. A small shivering girl
in a bedraggled pink swimsuit waves
to the engineer, a surfer puts down his board,
stands peeling off his black skin.

A man in sweats walks down the pier
pushing twins in a double stroller,
their heads nodding with each bump
over the worn wooden planks. One is asleep,
the other's eyes are open staring
into the cloudy sky. The wind
smells of french fries, pigeon poop,
and rotting kelp. The younger fisherman
pulls in his line, removes the bait, hooks
on a new and tastier piece. Counting Crows
replaces Green Day.

The other man shifts his weight,
glances at the lifeguard's Jeep
maneuvering down the pier.

There are 28,000 kinds of fish, he says,
but all I ever catch are these damn
perch. They're bony as all hell.
Global warming is going to put this pier
under water, just you wait and see.
One of these days we'll be fishing
for godknowswhat way up on El Camino.

Capricorn

He leans on the side of the building,
jeans barely clinging to his slender hips,
wispy hircine beard, just enough
to assert his Y chromosome. Lidded eyes
following girls' bare legs, hands
like Pan fingering his flute.
Bony chest, knobby wrists, lumps
on his forehead like budding horns.
Goat boy.

Fennel

When I was a kid we called it *finocchio*
and my mom bought it at the Italian grocery
or we picked it where it grew wild
in the empty lots of Los Angeles.
Now I buy it at my local market, the one
known for its gourmet stock.
They call it "sweet anise,"
I guess they think their customers
can't pronounce *finocchio.*
The other day a sweet, young thing
rang up my groceries,
"Oh," she said, swinging the soft, green plumes,
the sensuous white bulb,
into a plain brown paper bag,
"sweet anus."

Last Bus to Paradiso

I shall die, someday, on a tourist bus,
whose weary driver, bored
after three hundred thirty-four
trips to his particular wonder,
nods off for a nano-second
during sweet and lustful thoughts
of his girlfriend's luscious rump.

One day on the Transpeninsular two-laner,
Baja California Sur,
the speeding bus—broken seats,
open windows, swaying Virgin and all—
will hurtle to meet its twin head-on,
while passing uphill on a blind curve
with no third gear.

Or will the rear wheels slip and grab,
scrabbling furiously
in Norwegian mud as the driver guns
the engine, desperately and too late,
to escape our sudden sternward slide
into the freezing fingers
of Porsanger Fjord?

I think I would prefer
the Italian coast, where I'll make
a long, graceful, arcing plunge
from the brink of the Amalfi Drive
to join the bones
of some long-forgotten ancestor
who fished the ink and azure depths below.

Desire

doesn't work here anymore,
neither does Fancy. They went,
one after the other, many years ago.
Left me here to handle this place
alone, wash the dirty
plates, brew the bitter
coffee, sit sipping it
as the sun goes down.

Elegy for My 1958 Volkswagen

Beautiful blue beetle,
curved and dumpy, lovely
as a lumpy German *mädchen*
overly fond of *kartoffeln.*

Four cylinders chugging
in the rear, it was like being chased
by a busy washing machine.

Air-cooled engine slow
to warm my feet.
I loved how I could tuck it
into tiny San Francisco parking spots.

No gas gauge, just guess
the gas to get you there.
No synchromesh first gear,
no coasting through stop signs.

Small outside, it still thought big.
Record load—seven bags of groceries,
five kids, one friendly neighbor,
two dogs and a pair of bowling shoes.

I sold it. Never realizing
that it prophesied my life—
the inability to pass abruptly,
the slow fade on the long uphill grade.

Den Norske Amerika Linje

My husband sleeps beside me,
mumbling, twitching, dreaming again
of coming to *Amerika,* hurrying
through the streets of Oslo,
Kirkeveien to *Majorstuen*
to catch the *trikk* to the station
at *Nationalteatret.*

His *kuffert* falls open, spilling
clean shirts, pajamas, socks,
his good pair of *sko,* the leather
brown and shiny. He crams them
back, raises his hand
to hail a *drosje,* but the driver
drives past.

Han løper down the sidewalk
of *Rådhusgaten* all the way
to the docks at *Oslo Havn.*
He'll be too late, *for sent,*
for the ship. *Fort deg, fort deg,* hurry,
hurry, my beloved. You must
be on board the *Stavangerfjord.*
You must come to *Amerika*
and find me.

The Dream of Ahab

The sea haunted me for years before I saw it,
a slurry of smudges and haze,
the ultramarine of erasure.
My skies rose higher, an axis
of rotation on a counterweight
the night had strung with ancient stars.
Then the implausible fish blooming
from the depths, gliding
from the first flung shadows.
The water grows white, the great eye
rises, a memory
made from the body of the world.

Wildfire

Moon dismantled,
sun a red disk, reflecting

sea a rusty mudflat,
hot wind hollowing

canyons, hills littered
with dust, ash, soot,

chaparral, squirrels, palm trees,
shingles, Chevrolets, dictionaries,

wedding dress, quilt stitched
by a grandmother fifty years ago,

the bones of those who stayed,
the hopes of those who fled.

Close the windows.

Low Tide

A shiplike rock sails
upon its own shadow, prow
warty with anemones;
water, green and pale, wears
a scrim of foamy lace;
minnows dart from sun
to shadow to sun.

A single piece of kelp,
carved from amber, floats
gently in a shallow bowl; eelgrass
sways from a crevice, strands
abandoned in a mermaid's comb.

A hermit crab, lugging
his purloined home,
clambers from one spot
to another almost identical.
Barnacles stop kicking
food into their mouths, close
their shingles tightly against the heat.

Everything that lives
in these twin worlds
of water and of air
lies exposed.
The sky, shattered,
smiles back upon itself
in the green water.

The Midnight Horse

gallops through the night,
his hoofs striking stars
against the black,
his breath smoldering.
I can hear him
now, even in darkness.
Eight years it's been
since I came to this place,
riding on the back
of cells gone wild. Eight years
since I entered these roads
beyond roads beyond
roads. If he comes to me again,
how shall I greet him?

Pink Ribbons

Across from me
in the radiation waiting
room two women
work on a jigsaw puzzle.
They wear pink ribbons
for breast cancer.

I have a pink ribbon, too,
but I'm not wearing it.
The unfinished puzzle
lies on the table—pieces
of a bridge, bits
of improbably blue sky.

Calculus

Here, bury this.
Take it to the back yard
beneath the leaning pine. Scrape
away the deep-piled needles
with your bare hands.

Dig deep into the earth's moist
chill with the rusty spade
that was your mother's.
Remember her planting daffodils
until the hill sang yellow. Remember
the dementia. Remember

your fear of cells gone wild.
Remember the death
of the lilac in front of the house,
of the first man you married,
of the love you'd thought
would carry you.

When the hole is deep
and hungry, bury this thing. Never
think of it again.

For Purposes of Spirit Lifting

The seagull works as well as any other
bird. Better perhaps than the modest
brown towhee, head down, always pecking
at the ground. Certainly better
than the crow's black certainty.

Seagulls make it look easy, soaring
along the coast, riding storms aloft
and unperturbed. Or standing in flocks,
in clean white shirts,
always looking out to sea.

from
FLOUR, WATER, SALT

FutureCycle Press, 2016

Matins

Bread begins with the field,
with the grain bending its head
before the drifts and cracks
of wind and rain. It begins
with the yeast, blooming
in water warm as our bodies,
sugar, sweet as August heat.
Hands mixing flour,
water, salt, turning
the tendons of gluten
until they bend
to the will of the yeast.
Bake in the sun of the oven,
fill the house with praise.

Credo

I believe in fog drifting silently
from the Pacific Ocean,
in reading until my eyes burn,
I believe in the eyes of dogs, in wild rabbits,
in Beethoven's violin concerto,
in Joshua trees that stretch their arms
against a desert dawn.
I believe in not believing
in myth, nor in wishful thinking,
nor in a supernatural figure
who stirs things from above.
I believe in the smell of fresh-cut ginger
sunbaked kelp, orange blossoms
in hot August moonlight
and in the grace of dinner
beautifully prepared.

In Praise of Cinnamon Bread

Sliced and toasted, slathered
with cool yellow butter,
it wakes us to the morning
of possibility. Icing frosts
the top like the Sierra Nevada
in January. Inside, a swirl
of speckled brown spice,
the whirl of a galaxy
not yet encountered,
sprinkled with raisins
like a church of stars.

If I Were a Maker of Marzipan

I would propose love letters
be made only of marzipan roses,
lullabies of sweet marzipan apples,
invitations of marzipan oranges glowing
in the light of pleasant expectations.
Almonds to snare the sun, sugar
to sweeten the soul. The honeyed heart
of a fruity stollen, the pale green
shroud covering the indulgence
of a Swedish princess cake. The apples,
bananas, pears and pineapples of Sicily's
frutta Marturana. Aphrodisiac
of one night and a thousand. Taste.
If this isn't love, what is?

The Joy of Cooking

Tear down the walls
of your kitchen,
wear your apron tied
tight to hide the condiments
of rapture. Capture the wide
face of the moon
in your largest pot. Gather
the recollection of sunlight
upon the shoulders of young women.
There is no death when our teeth
crunch chicken bones, when our tongues
are slicked with yellow fat.
There is no death
when we lick our sticky lips.
There is love in milk
and salvation in the butter of heaven.

Feast

You are the papaya of my life,
sweet and juicy as August heat.
You are not cool as the salmon
splayed on a plate in the back
of the refrigerator, nor sour
as the lemon in its bright
untruthful skin. You are warm
and sweet, smooth as custard
scented with vanilla. Come
into my kitchen, love,
find the feather bed of good cooking.
Let me be the stocking
on your rolling pin, the slotted spoon
of longing. Together we will find
the measuring cup of desire.

Ode to the Toothpick

Not really tan, more like ecru,
fawn, tawny beige, presented
unshellacked and oddly

mismatched in a lidded box.
Shavings of thin veneer stamped
in clean tapered Bauhaus lines.

Singly they have no aroma,
but place your nose
to the small blue cardboard casket

and breathe the birch woods of Maine,
white-skinned, under a sky
of Botticelli blue.

Amulets

I buy oranges, tart and sweet,
skin thick enough
to ward off heartbreak, hives
and winter colds. Baskets
of bananas, yellow crescents
to remind me it is always warm
somewhere. Long, sturdy streaks of carrots
like flaming swords to ward off
dragons of despair. Blushing red,
crisp and sour, apples piled
like cobblestones to throw
against the loss of love.
A parsley boa, pearls of garlic,
a pale and monstrous cauliflower
to save me from myself.

Persimmons

What's to say?
It's hard to write a poem
about a fruit that's Dayglo orange
with sleek and slimy flesh
like summer gone rotten.
Persnickety I am, about their late
appearance on the stage,
when fall has pushed summer
to the wings, about their texture
of slugs, of blight, of a sickness
that shortens the days of August,
transforms them
into winter rain.

I Am an Apple on the Windowsill

I am orange blossoms in an August night,
printer's ink under the fingernails,
Cadmium Red and Cobalt Violet,
a field of wild mustard,
dark brown faded to white.

I am the palm frond sweeping the roof,
the coyote in the canyon,
a September fire,
unread pages in a borrowed book,
the silence between the waves.

I stand near the end of my years.
I stand without the aid of gods.
I sing when I can and cry when I can't.
I am a candle burned to evening.

Honeymoon

A rare steak in a Chinese restaurant
in Mexico City. What
got into me? The *tamales,*
the *Camarones a la Veracruzana,*

the *chilaquiles* with sour cream,
the *enchiladas verdes*
marking the hours of our trip
were not enough? Sick all night,

I lay in bed on the fifth floor
of the Gran Hotel. From the Zocolo.
only the random honk or swish of tires.
Finally he stirred and woke,

whispered to me of love, of his Norway,
of snow under the streetlights, of *fiskesuppe,*
of lamb and cabbage stew keeping comfort
in place on cold winter nights,

of the simmer of the two of us
starting our lives over,
dredged in the flour of expectation,
marinated in hope.

Sustenance

I take the roast out of the refrigerator.
It's a small one, all we need,
now that the children are grown.
I lay a couple of cloves of garlic
on the cutting board
and hit them hard with the flat of my knife.
The papery skin pops off,
and the cloves crack open.

I go out into the garden
and cut a handful of Italian parsley,
make slits in the roast,
stuff them with garlic and parsley,
rub the roast with olive oil,
roll it in cracked pepper.

I put the roast on the barbecue
along with a few red potatoes
rubbed with olive oil. I lower the lid
and go into the house to make the salad.
My husband comes to set the table.
While we wait for the roast to cook,
we sit at either end of the couch, reading.

When it's time,
I put the roast and potatoes
on the old blue and white platter.
My husband opens a bottle of Chianti.
I toss the salad, he lights the candles.
We sit across from each other and eat.
Under the table,
my bare feet rest on top of his.

Aubade with French Toast

Fog obscures the house across
the street, blurs the eucalyptus
towering above the church,
smudges the blues of the ocean.
A scattering of crows swims mute
through thickened air. I've opened

the bag of bread and it's gone stale.
What's left but to make French toast?
Milk cooler than the sky, eggs
beaten creamy and pale.
Hardened bread soaked
to a second life. A pan with butter.

Air and fog sift together
like flour and water
in this wakening world.
Mornings are best taken on faith.
Don't ask for more.

Ode to Sardines

The northern sea,
immaculate and immense,
drops anchor
on my kitchen counter.
Moonlight reassembled
as layers of watered silk
head to tail
in a bright tin coffin.

Woman Washing Dishes

—after Christopher Merrill

After dinner, alone now, passing plates,
left hand to right, tipping them under
running water, sluicing fragments
of food to the bottom of the sink,

putting away leftovers, closing
the refrigerator, holding a bowl,
two forks together, another
bowl, stacking it all in the dishwasher.

Turns the water to hot, takes the big blue pot,
then the small one, scours them,
picks up the cast-iron pan, scrubs
at charred remainders, scrapes them off,

dumps them onto the pile rinsed
from the plates, sweeps
it all toward the disposal,
turns on the water, hard,

and the remains of the last meal
they have eaten together
whirl around the sink, and down.

Hard Dreams

A long row of them unattended,
afire with our history.
The year we went to Senegal,
the summer we used my father's spade
to bury the dog, the throne
we built in the oak tree.
All of these just tangles
in the fringe of time.

The summer when the roses died,
wild thorns at the edge of the skies,
tangerines glowing uselessly
on a white ceramic plate,
bread leavened with the soil
of our own want.
The honey these have left us
may never be unbittered.

A Recipe for Loss

The funeral begins
with the melancholy of roses cut
from the axis that connects
them to the earth. With the music
of forfeiture, the prayers
of nothing-to-be-done,
the gathering of the lost
around the table—the ham,
potato salad, baked beans,
green rings of Jell-O,
coconut cake with melancholy
built into every layer. The wife
in her black dress.

Garage Sale

The waffle iron she got as a wedding present
in 1951. Frayed cord, baked-on grime.
Tubes of oil paints, twisted, missing
labels. Without screwing off the cap,
who's to know thalo green from cobalt blue?
Three pink bouillon cups, four saucers.
A dainty blue eggcup, pale as an April sky,
only a tiny chip on the edge. Diamonds?
Got to be rhinestones. Old Reader's
Digest books, boxes of National Geographic,
The Joy of Cooking. Ladle,
can opener, measuring spoons.
One adult tricycle, a battered walker,
sixty-four jelly jars waiting for spring.

Dinner Is Served

—Most women who go mad, go mad in kitchens. Judith Newton

I am building evidence
in the absence a recipe.
Pages are missing,
the knife is dull as celery.
The refrigerator holds only curdled
milk, wilted lettuce
and three old eggs. And radishes.
I could make you a necklace
of overage radishes, dark and peppery.
I think of hotcakes on a bed of onions.
What I find is a bottle opener wed
to a cheese grater gone rusty.
I would place dinner on the empty
table—caviar with custard,
fish swimming in maple syrup,
a salad of eucalyptus leaves—
but my kitchen offers only
a burned-out mixer, a dented
set of measuring spoons, and a roasting
fork which threatens my life.

The Real Story

In a kitchen where the ceiling
is extremely low, the heat
from the pan of frying chicken
almost melts the rafters.
Nuts and raisins cuddle
in the muesli. Lettuce leaves
the comfort of the refrigerator,
flaps its wings, flies around the lamp.
Cans of tuna and tomatoes
creep from the pantry to make
extended love under the table.
Wine consorts with beer
to no good end. The steam
from the boiling kettle
fills the room with a promise
false as cream. The man
who comes to eat
will break your heart.

The Moon's an Empty Fruit

Pale as an onion, an orange
with the color sucked out,
a bleached and naked kiwifruit,
an apple with a pockmarked skin,
a damaged sphere that has never
contained what we've ascribed
to it, the hopes of lovers, the light
for our dark nights, a guidebook
for lost and weary travellers. Hanging
improbably above us it threatens
to ripen, to fall to earth,
soft and rotten, a turnip
without a blush.

This Explains Why the Chicken Suit You Always Wear for Work Is So Damn Hot

—a Google cento

Cook the damn chicken cutlets woman,
        don't eat 'em raw!

Motherfucker got the bone
all the way out the damn chicken.

Free dating. Singles and Personals.
Best Damn Chicken Wings ever.

Erotic is using a feather, kinky
is using the whole damn chicken.

Damn chicken pocks, I'm gonna get it.
I swear I'm gonna kill him.

I need those chicken pills
so i can wear my applebottom jeans next week.

Come, eat your dinner.

Self Service

Irish stew, mashed potatoes,
spinach, sliced tomatoes.
Steam tables, shining chrome,
servers waiting, green beans,
buttered bread, people puddling
behind, Jell-O, chocolate pudding.
Can I change my mind, exchange
the meat loaf for roast beef? Go back
to pick up pickled tongue? Return
the doll I stole from Kresge's in 1944?
Oatmeal cookies, coconut cakes,
dates, roommates, jobs, chicken, baked.
Can I slip my first husband back
among the lemons? If I return
to get creamed peas, I might
decide they're not for me.
The line behind is getting longer.
My second husband's waiting
near the angel cake. Now
the line in front is shorter
than the line behind.
I'm getting closer to the end,
to the place I'll have to pay
for everything
that's on my tray.

Going Home

When you come to the fork in the road
lean down and pick it up. Turn it over
in your hands, notice if it is silver or stainless
steel. Is it well used? Tines bent? Handle
skewed? Do you recognize the pattern? Raise
your head, look down the road, take the turn
that leads to the house with lights on,
roast chicken, bright with juice,
mother removing her apron.

from
NO LONGER AT THIS ADDRESS

Kelsay Press, Aldrich Books, 2017

At the Cabin

Sunshine, and smoke
from fires to the north, meet
over the mountains as if
for the first time. Breeze
shimmers through aspens, haze
dissipates, reappears.

A hummingbird buzzes
towards afternoon. Some other bird
sings beyond the leaves.
Beneath faded eaves, carpenter bees
tunnel to rest, to reappear, all of this
prompting the day.

The sprinkler mists
the grass, a single squirrel
rests in a patch of warmth.
All is sunshine and smoke
weighted against the edge
of morning.

Solitaire

The leaves of Tuesday will be gone by three
to their life without shadows.
My mother shuffles from room to room.
Teacups are soon empty.

In her life without shadows,
my mother searches for her keys.
Her teacup is soon empty.
The hanging chimes are still.

My mother searches for her keys,
but they've been gone for years.
The hanging chimes are still.
In an old house there is no air,

it's been gone for years.
Four birds have hit the glass this fall.
Near an old house there is no air,
there is no rising of new grass.

Four birds have hit the glass this fall.
My mother shuffles from room to room.
There is no rising of new grass.
The leaves of Tuesday will be gone by three.

After Everything Else

The weight of the final
picking of winter pears
lies golden
on the table. The last
of the last rain
drips from the eaves.
Three wild rabbits edge
onto the lawn, round brown
eyes alert.

Across the street,
a man in overalls, teetering
on the ultimate edge
of age, carries his hoe
into the sun. The white cat
picks its way along the curb
lifting its head
at a sound I can't hear.

Elegy for My Mother

It seemed she was always standing
between the door and the west moon,
wearing a soiled shirt and old shoes.
Rusted rasps and chisels, the calendar
with notes scribbled
in her diminished hand,
the fragile vehicle of her skull,
that ruined house,
entirely too large for what was left.
Eleven years she has been ashes
spun where stones lie still
beneath the sun on Mohawk Hill.

At the Door

He kneels to God
on a pile of broken dishes
where light pours
onto the white floor.
An old man, his radio fades
as he moves farther and farther
from town. He remembers
storms lit by stars, bluebonnets
in the back yard, tomatoes
warm from the sun.
The clock in the corner
tolls three. Soon,
they will dismantle
this place
and carry him away.

Beyond the Waves

When I was very small, and didn't yet
know how to swim, my mother
used to take me out beyond the waves.

The waves were sometimes big and strong,
the water dark and deep, but I was safe
as long as Mother held my hand.

She's several years past ninety now,
and here in the mountains,
far from the sea, she keeps watch.

The trees might fall,
she warns me, they are so tall,
and there are so many of them.

Faces

Sometimes I see old high school friends
walking down the street and hurry
after them only to discover
they've disappeared into someone else.
Once I spied my former college roommate
buying a baguette in Paris, a copy
of Le Monde tucked under her arm.

Then there was that freezing day
in April, 1988, when I rode the up escalator
out of the Moscow subway, only to catch sight
of my ex-husband, going down.

It must be that there are only so many faces
in the world, and the longer we live,
the more familiar they become.
Just yesterday, I came upon a little man,
with thinning grey hair and a moustache,

alone in the supermarket. He put a single jar
of Dundee Orange Marmalade
into his empty basket, then turned away,
pushing his cart down the aisle, leaving me

clutching my own jar of Dundee, and watching
my father, twelve years after his death,
disappear around the baked goods and batteries
toward the checkout stand.

Meadow Vista

There is a window facing west,
a woman staring beyond the tree,
she does not remember why.
A peeling chair among the weeds.

A woman staring beyond the tree,
turning pages in a book she can no longer read.
A peeling chair among the weeds,
a green glass globe that didn't break.

Turning pages in a book she can no longer read,
her stubby fingers seek a place.
The green glass globe that didn't break
is placed just so, against the light.

Her stubby fingers seek a place
that will make sense, that she can know.
Placed just so, against the light,
a picture taken when she was young

will make sense that she can know.
She does not remember why.
In a picture taken when she was young
there is a window facing west.

Crossing on Red

Gray morning, traffic light.
Just as it turns green,
a motorcycle policeman stops
in the middle of the intersection.

Tan shirt, brown pants, heavy gloves,
stomach bulging over thick black belt.
He stands spraddle-legged, holds up
his hands, palms out.

A white hearse crosses, followed
by a long line of cars. Red light.
The cars keep coming, rusty VW,
faded station wagon, old maroon sedan.

Green light. I drum my fingers, wonder
who died. A skinny teenager bops along
the curb, flailing his arms. In the car
next to me a woman puts on lipstick.

The last of the procession crosses
the intersection. Red light. I wait.
Only the dead and those who grieve
can cross on the red light.

Entropy

"Stick by stick,"
my father used to say,
"stone by stone."
The roof develops leaks,
the water heater dies,
the olive tree
heaves the bricks of the patio
into humps and ridges.
Mileage accumulates
on cars that seldom leave the garage.

Each day another layer of fiber
wears from the carpet in the hall,
the contraption in the toilet tank,
creaks closer toward collapse,
the children,
playing in the yard only yesterday,
begin to show white hair.
The furnace
goes bang in the night.

Spiders in the Bathtub

I arrive late,
fall into musty sheets,
wake early, moon fading
like the tender flesh of a rotting apple.
She hadn't a clock in the house.
In the loft, a mouse's fairy skeleton.

Fishing line in tangles on the workbench,
four work gloves laid in a row, none matching,
an empty can of Liquid Wrench. The last
of her clay sculptures abandoned in the dust.
The spread of meadow is clenched by light.

Afternoon white and silent as iron,
not a breath to move the pines. A hawk
sails silent overhead. Wasps
hide in the heat like words unspoken,
She is one of the invisible upon the mountain.
All lives are mutual. Love is not enough.

Fire, Fire

Clouds of smoke,
ten times the width

of the twice-grown canyon,
tides of reddish brown

tugged like boats upstream
from the blowing blaze.

Riverbeds of incineration,
islands of dry grass, frightening

beachheads afloat in the dark.
Slopes tangled in fishnets of flame.

Look to roof!

Keys

She's outside early this morning,
meandering around the yard,
legs pale and bare beneath

her short red bathrobe, feet stuck
into an old pair of slippers
that used to belong to my father.

She pauses in the backyard under
the oak tree, a strand of sun
touching her white hair.

Yesterday we brought her back to her house
in Meadow Vista. She didn't want
to stay long at her cabin in the mountains.

"The river's no good for swimming any more,
and they've cut down so many trees.
Besides, all my friends are dead."

But here at home the screen door is broken,
her favorite clippers need to be sharpened,
the light bulb on the porch is burned out.

One minute, she talks of leaving
and going to live in one of those places.
The next, she says she'd rather die.

Now she's wandering from one door
to another—workshop, front door, side door, workshop,
then over to the garage apartment.

Finally, she comes into the house,
stands in the middle of the carpet
in muddy slippers.

Dangling from her fingers is not her key chain
but my husband's. "I have all these keys,"
she says, "but I can't make them fit anything."

First Light

White sand turned damp
at water's brim. Waves defeated
by the shore. All those
in graves where grass
is cut too short. All
poems of morning
that never get it right.
Clouds rimmed with pink,
light from the east, all these,
and radios, gathered
here around the edge
of morning.

Hide and Seek

Time fools my mother.
Sometimes she is ten years old
on Long Island, and thinks
that I am with her, both of us
running through the house,
climbing out her bedroom window
to sneak across the roof,
knocking croquet balls
"clear to Halifax."

She is growing backwards,
and I am chasing her,
panting through the gardens,
crunching down the gravel drive
past the rhododendrons. Always,
just when I think I've caught her,
she disappears around another corner.

In the Forest

Who owns all these trees?
asks my mother, pointing
with a finger warped by arthritis.
Who plants them?

See way up on that tall tree?
She pulls at the bandage
under her arm where
they took the biopsy.

The branches all stop
at the exactly same place.
Who trimmed them?

Doesn't lightning ever strike them?
Why don't they fall in the wind?
How did they get so old?

Dementia

My mother's purse,
almost empty,
brass clasp gaping open,
shredded tissues,
cracked mirror,
black lining,
no keys inside.

Late September

and still so much to do—
the bending over the bowl
of dough, the mending
of socks worn through the toe,
the paring of peaches, lovely
in their waning.

Statice beyond the glass, lusterless,
like fog against a window, fading
purple blossoms dry
as paper. Dusk is brittle
on my shoulders. I will leave
as I came in, already falling.

No Longer at This Address

Another letter for Aunt Katie today,
Sisters of the Little Flower requesting
funds. Seven years dead and still
the mail arrives—announcement
from the Italian Center, application
from a home for the aged,
postcard misdirected.

The Brinkster's beagle is loose again;
Mrs. Newman's petunias
are a tumble of color; a package
sits on the stoop next door.
I close the mailbox,
turn toward the house.

The mail truck rumbles toward town,
the kid on the bicycle
pedals around the corner,
the bricks of the driveway
turn dark with rain,
and the dead die slowly.

The Shirt

In the dressing room
I tell my mother to take off her shirt.
"I don't understand why we're here,"

she says. I explain again about the cancer,
and hang her shirt on the hook.
"Whose shirt is that?" she asks.

After the X-rays, we go back
to the dressing room. She looks
at the shirt on the hook.

"Where did that come from?"
"It's yours," I say, and hand it to her.
"Why am I here?" she asks again.

"To see about the cancer."
"I don't have cancer," she says.
"And this is not my shirt."

Christmas Snapshots

The year the tree fell down.
The year he came home safe.
Visiting aunts, sleepy, their hair in curlers.
World War II and plastic ornaments
because the glass kind came from Germany.
The year of chocolate coins in all our stockings.
The year of Uncle Jim, drunk and jubilant,
wavering at the head of the stairs,
my crippled grandmother in his arms.

The year the tree blew over.
The year I moved back home to wait.
Slippers again, for everyone.
The tiny tree in San Francisco
because the apartment was so small.
The year of the first grandchild.
The year of my mother, a startled animal,
under the arm of the Santa
from Meals on Wheels.

A Song on the End

First there will be your darkening heart
beating against misleading light
as if startled by shellfire.
You will burn like opening breath,
contain fire without flinching.
As birds remember snow
under a column of sky, you
will remember the feel of the path.
Sixty years to the coast,
it's easy as whistling.

from
WHAT'S LEFT OVER

FutureCycle Press, 2022
Winner of the FutureCycle Poetry Book Prize

Enough

Too many streets in this city, with their spines
drawn white, their paving black
as loss. As many as the branches
of winterbare sycamores
leading away from home. As many
as the veins that trace their course
through our bodies. Central Avenue,
broad and straight, leads directly
to the beating heart of downtown. Sunset
Drive takes you to the aging painted ladies
and their scrolls of gingerbread trim.
There's the avenue of cancer, the boulevard
of diabetes, the irregular lane following
fibrillation of the heart, the wandering
way of dementia with its bridge broken
over the river of self.

And the Rivers Shall Run into the Sea

Night leaves earlier now,
the dark bleeding away
from the horizon as day,
in its thin summer cloak,
lifts a field of sky
over slopes of wild mustard
eaten by light.

But summer is pregnant
with the raking light of fall,
a somber gold etching
the city into bright and dark.

And fall is reborn into winter
with its dark run of shadows up the valley,
faster now, faster,
relentlessly turning, relentlessly
opening the door.

Occultation

The clock never chimes seven. Sundown
seeps from heavens to horizon.

The teakettle's misplaced its song,
succor runs dry as an empty cup.

Songbirds lost to the sky, doves, mockingbirds
and the one forever undiscovered.

The photograph of our wedding day,
colors smeared into the background trees.

The contracture of my husband's crippled fingers,
as he lies sleeping in the singing heat.

Years ago, we flew to Paris, hauled our luggage
with the broken wheel around the corners of happiness.

How many days did it take to arrive here?
A grayfly crawls up the wall, slower than summer.

In Your 86th Year

There isn't much left
of the potato salad
and there is no more roast.
Our supply of coffee beans
is running low. Library
books are overdue.
The photo of you on my desk,
so young, with such dark
wavy hair, has faded.
Morning glories, blue
in the afternoon sun,
are closing. The cherries,
so dark, so sweet, are almost gone.
Hurry, grab the last few.

Coming to Winter

I've spent this winter listening,
for the tapping fingers of rain
on the skylight, the unexplained
electronic chirp that haunts
the kitchen, the gurgle
of pea soup on the back
burner. I've turned my ear
toward the windup groan
of the sphygmomanometer,
the sound of my husband's breath
in the night, the whine of the dog
next door who's ever hopeful for the return
of the one who won't return.

A Celestial Shift

Every year the skies are higher
and the moon reels farther and farther away
to hang among stars younger than the sun.

The earth will unseal a sparkling trail
like a cauterized incision
assembled by light. The tides

will cease, lovers will fumble
for each other in the dark,
day will diminish

until it sinks into stasis.
A crow flaps onto a telephone pole.
A cockroach scuttles across the kitchen floor.

Happiness

If it should come,
lie down with it,
breathing I am so glad
you're here,

each word
a fisherman
casting letters
onto the sea.

Let it come
like a song unto grass,
the entanglement
of what is outside

and what is held within.
Hold it cupped
in your palms
like a bruised gentian.

Sommer

In Norway they have a saying
I fjor falt sommeren på en torsdag.
Last year summer fell on a Thursday.

Summer, when the temperatures reach
a torrid 75 degrees, the balconies
of houses and apartments are festooned
with quilts hung out to air, and women
on park benches unbutton their shirts
to soak in the thin northern sun.

Summer, when the flower boxes
on every window burst with
open-throated petunias in every color,
and the sun shines and shines
as if to make up for time lost
in winter's dark and cold.

Summer it was, when I was there,
and sailed with the love of my life
on a sailboat on the Oslo fjord,
stopping at a friend's island *hytte*
for wild raspberries and cream.

And when we docked, the sun
at midnight, at midnight, at midnight.
Oh, the midnight sun.

July Morning

Puzzle pieces of bright blue sky slip
through the branches of the magnolia.
Sun glints on its polished leaves,
turns them into patches of silver.
Across the canyon someone is building
a deck. Bang, bang, bang.

The Labrador retriever next door,
barks once and is answered
by a thin, high yip several backyards away.
Wistaria shifts slightly in a breath of breeze.
A single lavender blossom floats,

spiraling down
to rest on the empty birdbath.
Beside me, my husband rolls over
and runs his fingers
along the curve of my hip.

Three Minute Love Song

Headlights
flash across the dark,
the garage door squeaks,
sticks in the middle,
shuts with a double thump.
The padlock rattles,
against the wood,
the gate squeals
on its hinges,
the patio door
slides open.

The Nomenclature of Desire

The name of the lily
is the name I had before
I was born. Before white,
before red, before the moon
carved itself into one thin hair.
The name of the sea
is salt and spray
and flat blue under pale.
My lover's name is written
on my palm. The name
of the grass is always.

Love in Our Eighth and Ninth Decades

It's like lifting a violin out of its case,
a trick of the light that drives the music.
We give ourselves to these well-known melodies
as if our bodies were as they were before,
and our hearts slide into the world of sheer delight
where we tangle ourselves
in every way we're still able,
glut our mad old eyes with each other,
until everything is reduced to a single light.
Our skin glistered in sweat,
we can be beautiful again.

Liquefied by Light

A gap in leaden clouds develops
above a horizon full of ghosts.
It reveals the tissue of the lost,
just as the arrow of the compass
reels to find its resting place.
The imperfect past, grey as a glacier,
circles in sequence
with the hiss of waves. Light
is an echo of an echo crashing
into stars. The tides unspool themselves.
A seagull lifts, and then is gone.

Sky, Interrupted

The invisible light of lilacs floats
in waves above the garden. Sparrows

paint the roses white, dye the lilies
the color of loss. The olive tree weeps

for its leaves. Iris and peonies slouch
in the sun. After a long tomorrow,

when the hose lies unattended,
and the iron gate has been repaired,

the disoriented dead will fold their hearts
and settle upon the waiting grass.

Sometimes

My heart is air. I breathe it in
and it smells of sorrow.
It is a lemon on the tree
they gave me when he died.
It is brown like his eyes
and tastes of sugar and salt.
Sometimes I am heavy
with love. Sometimes
it's just a memory.

Apology to My Body

I'm sorry for those cups of strong coffee
downed at all hours of the day and night.

For the countless cans of tuna fish, laced
with mayonnaise, pickles, and mercury.

For the carcinogens of spareribs
blackened over fuming coals.

I'm sorry for long lazy afternoons in a chair
by the window, gazing at the ocean

writing poems in my head, while others
walked briskly along the edge of the surf.

For skipping the water exercises because I hated
getting dressed in the damp and noisy locker room.

For sitting on the deck at the cabin, reading
instead of hiking for a view into the distance.

For having developed a craving
for carbohydrates and fat. The bland richness

of mashed potatoes and butter. Ice cream
and cookies and pie. The sweetness

that's gone out of my life since he died.

I Can't Remember

There were only your breaths, gasping
now, the music of death flowing
through the afternoon, the sunlight
silent in the air. I held your hand
under the sheet. I can't remember
who was there. I can't remember
what I wore. I can't remember
when your hand grew cold.

Incognito

Clothespins are birds
clinging to the line in the yard.
Try to find a walking stick insect
on a dead tree. The leaf mantis
cleverly imitates, you guessed it, a leaf.
There's a bird that sings like my cell phone.
I see a discarded bicycle chain
near the trashcan, and it's a rattlesnake.
A hammer in the distance barks
like a watchdog. The clink
of the icemaker is my husband,
dead for a year, seeking
a late-night snack.

Still Life with Tax Return

Paperwork from Social Security
and the Norwegian pension.

Yellow highlighter smudged with ink,
calculations on the backs of unfinished
poems, sphygmomanometer.

Thick pile of medical expenses—
doctors, prescriptions, cremation.

Records of donations—his shirts,
six pairs of pajamas, faded jeans,
his astronomy books, his favorite shoes.

Empty stapler, broken box of paperclips.
Cup of coffee grown bitter, no sugar.

Almost There

She worked her roster of duties,
stood watch instead of sleeping.
She made it past the days
she gave him sips of water from a spoon,
navigated the shoals of his failing
and regaining, weathered his sinking
through August into fall.
Now she's unloaded the ballast
of shirts and shoes he left
behind, swum through the black
of nights without solace, of dawns
that brought no light.
Her ship is nearing port. Alone
is what she's learning.
She's almost there.

OTHER POEMS

After Everything Else

The weight of the final
picking of winter pears
lies golden
on the table. The last
of the last rain
drips from the eaves.
Three wild rabbits edge
onto the lawn, round brown
eyes alert.

Across the street,
a man in overalls, teetering
on the ultimate edge
of age, carries his hoe
into the sun. The white cat
picks its way along the curb
lifting its head
at a sound I can't hear.

Corpus

This body, this boat I've sailed on
for over eighty years. This boat
that passed so surely over the turbulence
of my teens—new breasts, new hips,
new emotions slipping restraint.

This body that carried the passengers
that were my daughter and my son.
This dinghy that let one marriage
slip but held the other in the measured
calm of a safe harbor. This body
with its cargo of days in the sun, of nights
guided by the twin stars of hope and ignorance.

This body that twice bore me past the shoals
of angry cells run amok, that weathered
a heart that swung in irregular cadences.
This body now bends and pulls and creaks,
gathering pain and stiffening joints,
the indignity of leaks. This vessel, this cruiser,
this liner heading for the unknown deep.

Coyote

Coyote roams his home
in the hills surrounding
the town, lifts his nose

from the gloom laid down
on ground dark
as the heart of a crow,

roams where the bones
of the moon loom
over the hollow,

tosses song
and moonlonging to the glow
overhead, lopes through sere chaparral,

red-barked manzanita, scrub oak,
wild tobacco drooping over dust,
spikey yucca's candled blooms,

creeps from hill to canyon to valley
where the city grows like Mexican broom
swarming up the arroyo. Alone

in my own garden Coyote drinks
from the fountain, stops

on the low stone wall
throws his eyes to the sky
and the deep black wells

of their centers hold a light
white as bone.

Disobedience

I will wake the lilies under
the window. I will bite deeply
into the apple's defenseless cheek.
I will follow the seagulls over
the waves as they etch the air
with their wings. I will not
be good. I will not be safe.
I will ride the tide as it goes out.
And when the man comes in the dark,
I will show him the family
silver's shining secrets.

Fishermen at Night

So many lights, scattered
like forget-me-nots across the dark sea.
They could be reflected stars
but the sky is clouded over. The sun,
like an old fox, has disappeared
into its dark den, and the moon has yet
to creep over Cristianitos Ridge.

Do the men on those little boats
call out to each other
in encouragement, do they argue
about who took the best spot, banter
about the Dodgers' last game?

I have faith in fish and in the multitude
of creatures that live beneath membrane
of the ocean. Little boats, just past the breakers,
it matters what you catch,
it matters that fishermen get older
and their faces change.

Jesus in a Jacket

Fourth of July came early
the year that I was ten,
brought on by the heat, they said.
Uncle came to the picnic
wearing a jacket and tie.

"Nobody," he said, "knows more
about the stock market. Nobody,"
he said, "can give you better advice."
He folded his hands over his vest
and the red stone in his ring
flashed in the sun.

The little girl who didn't have a nickname
wanted that ring for her own.
Uncle smiled, swore it would be hers
if she could take it from his finger.
Pazzo, pazzo, pazzo.

She tugged at the ring, twisted it,
pulled it toward his big, pink knuckle,
until finally, she pulled it off,
held it warm and glowing
on her palm.

My uncle with the soft white hair,
my uncle, who knew God
and the market, and the ways of men,
reached out his soft, pale, fleshy hand
and took it back.

Learning Pain

—after Howard Nemerov

Before you can learn pain, you must learn
the language of pain. The words are easy.
They turn out not to be foreign after all.
You've heard them all your life.
Breathe deeply, this won't hurt,
she's gone, he's been committed.

Worse are the words that have shaped the pain—
embolism, coronary thrombosis, metastasis,
no survivors, divorce decree,
she's killed herself, three months at best.

Once you've understood all this,
you will go into the world to see
if its tortured streets correspond
to what you've learned. Not well at all,

it turns out. The pain of your divorce
may differ from that of another's separation.
Must you learn to experience
an average parting?

Example—in the book on grief and dying
death spews itself in coils
around your throat. In reality, it may
instead pyramid upon your chest.

Maybe it's not cancer. Dreadful hope.
It may be weeks before you see results,
Or months. Or years.

Still, little by little you will start to learn
the way pain cuts across the world,
always at the worst location,
how learning its infinite varieties
changes only you, and not the pain.

Luftwaffe

The storm
comes for the throat,

a sidewinder in darkness.
Wind works its mutinies

in storm-snarled trees. Water
hammers houses from their roots,

a bus shoots under a bridge.
A man in a tattered T-shirt

floats downriver like a page
torn from a book.

Malediction for a Neighbor

May you choke on the air
you let out of our tires. May the poison
you poured onto our pink oleander
seep into your drinking water, creep
to corrode your closets of collected guns.
Let there be termites, moths, cracks,
paint that peels, sagging gutters.
Let an unprecedented hurricane rip off the roof
that ruined the view for those across the street.
Let the leaves from our trees scatter
onto your plastic grass. May something
large go bang in the night.

And as the moving truck pulls away
I give thanks to the Gods of Foreclosure
and pray that the Spirit-of-Lose-Your-Shirt
follows you from run-down housing tract
to tacky apartment, to trailer park to tent.
Amen.

Ode to Stillness

Praise to the stillness when the baby falls asleep,
a milky pearl suspended from his bottom lip,
to the silence when the yapping dog
gives up and curls into the shade,
to the goldfish circling his glassy walls.

Honor the moment between
the shore-churned waves,
the hour of dawn when the cricket
folds his legs at last. Praise
the silence of the sun's yellow light,
clouds accumulating in the west.

Wait for three am, when at last he sighs,
turns over in bed and stops snoring.
Step into the still and silent air
after last wisp of the Santa Ana
has swept the canyon. Praise again
to the rose and the morning glory
and the magnolia
motionless in morning fog.

Old women in beauty parlors

arrange themselves,
balancing gently,
each step a questioning
of bony hips seeking
the arch of youth. In love

with the architecture of trembling
blue curls circling sparsely
over pink scalps, leaning back
in black plastic chairs,
ammonia fumes shuddering

the air, they hum along
with Muzak while with blue-veined
fingers they hand rollers to Michael,
or Erik or Janelle. As their clocks
move toward midnight,
and the kitchen is wiped clean,

they remember singing
with the radio of a parked
Pontiac coupe. Do they
still tremble with lust,
or just roll away, heads wrapped
in tissue against the curls of desire?

Spell to Name the Unnameable

Light small fires against the screen
that separates close from distant.

Petition the sea tern to spin the compass,
the horse to silhouette the sky.

Burn mushrooms, magazines,
and mayberries salted with stars.

Balance rainbow upon rainbow
until there is no trace of longing,
no residue of what was lost.

Follow the red clay road
over the hill to an unspecified town
where the houses are unnumbered

and the answer lies buried
under the doorstone.

Leave
your footprints leading away.

Stargazers

Lilies strain from the mouth
of the vase by the window, open

their throats to the sky, stretching
toward the accumulation of clouds,

furred stamens powdered red
as starling's blood. The shadows

of the room, the scent of
perfume heavy as tomorrow's end

held in stasis for seven steady
days as stems collapse in secret

and leaves transmute to slime.
In this world of sorrow and of loss

all things must fail, must come to moss
and murder, must disintegrate

in damp and dust. And we must
open our throats, and swallow.

The hearts of horses

the ears of cats,
the tails of dogs following
their masters home.

The love of old husbands,
for their old wives, the way
they move closer in the night.

The Season of Dogs

The Dalmatian
in the concrete pen
barks and barks and
barks again. This

is the season of dogs,
a lark of barks, a powwow
of yowls, the canicular chorus
of the fox terrier

in the tract mansion
and the dachshund
next door who never shuts up.
Even old Schnitz, grizzled

and gray, behind
the tall pink wall, cannot resist.
The oaks stand black against
the sky. The moon looms

by the water tower. On the other side
of the canyon someone
pulls a shade
across a lighted window.

Acknowledgments

American Journal of Poetry: "Malediction for a Neighbor"
As It Ought To Be: "Disobedience," "Stargazers," "Spell to Name the Unnameable"
Atlanta Review: "Last Bus to Paradiso"
Atticus Review: "The hearts of horses," "Love in Our Eighth and Ninth Decades"
Barefoot Review: "The Midnight Horse"
Blue Heron Review: "Ode to Stillness"
Clockhouse Review: "Spiders in the Bathtub"
Connecticut River Review: "Meadow Vista"
Cultural Daily: "Corpus"
Hanging Loose: "The Shirt"
IthacaLit: "Coyote," "Enough," "And the Rivers Shall Run into the Sea"
Kentucky Review: "Elegy for My Mother"
Misfit Magazine: "I Can't Remember"
Muddy River Poetry Review: "Fishermen at Night"
Naugatuck River Review: "Jesus in a Jacket"
Nerve Cowboy: "Fennel"
Nimrod: "Afghanistan," "At the Door"
North American Review: "Ode to the Toothpick," "Ode to Sardines"
Plainsong: "Calculus"
Poetry New Zealand: "Sustenance"
Poetry East: "Three Minute Love Song," "Hide and Seek"
Poetry Quarterly: "Old women in beauty parlors," "Poured Melting from the Dark," "What Is Left to Show That I Was Here?"
Rattle: "Elegy for My 1958 Volkswagen"
RE:AL: "Dementia"
Red Paint Hill: "Dinner Is Served"
Rhino: "Sixty-Seven years"
Sheila-Na-Gig: "Learning Pain," "The Nomenclature of Desire"
Slant: "Self Service"
Spillway: "First Light"
Sugar House Review: "The Season of Dogs," "Fire, Fire"
Tar River Poetry: "After Everything Else"
10x3 Plus: "Wildfire"
Untitled Country Review: "West of Reno"
Verse Wisconsin: "Late September," "Settling Accounts"
Voices in Italian America: "Sewing Lessons"
Word Soup: "Going Home"
The Writer: "Red"
Zone International Journal of Prose and Poetry: "Luftwaffe"

"Faces" appeared in *Twelve Los Angeles Poets (Onthebus Poets)*, published by Bombshelter Press, 2002.

About FutureCycle Press

FutureCycle Press is dedicated to publishing lasting English-language poetry in both print-on-demand and Kindle formats. Founded in 2007 by long-time independent editor/publishers and partners Diane Kistner and Robert S. King, the press was incorporated as a nonprofit in 2012. A number of our editors are distinguished poets and writers in their own right, and we have been actively involved in the small press movement going back to the early seventies.

Each year, we have awarded the FutureCycle Poetry Book Prize and honorarium for the best original full-length volume of poetry we published that year. Introduced in 2013, our Good Works projects benefit various charities. Our Selected Poems series highlights contemporary poets with a substantial body of work to their credit; with this series we strive to resurrect work that has had limited distribution and is now out of print.

We are dedicated to giving all of the authors we publish the care their work deserves, offering a catalog of the most diverse and distinguished work possible, and paying forward any earnings to fund more great books. All of our books are kept "alive" and available unless and until an author asks that their book be taken out of print.

We've learned a few things about independent publishing over the years. We've also evolved a unique and resilient publishing model that allows us to focus mainly on vetting and preserving for posterity poetry collections of exceptional quality without becoming overwhelmed with bookkeeping and mailing, fundraising activities, or taxing editorial and production "bubbles." To find out more, come see us at futurecycle.org.

www.ingramcontent.com/pod-product-compliance
Lightning Source LLC
Chambersburg PA
CBHW072145090426
42739CB00013B/3282